30 |

WAKE UP AND WIN

Version 1

Tammy Price

TWTT Enterprises

Contents

PREFACE

I am Tammy "Tammy with the Tea" Price; I was in a very dark place two and a half years ago. I was in a really dark depression after losing everything and everybody. I started a health and wellness business and met Stormy Wellington, who is the Visionary of the Wake Up and Win call every Monday through Friday at 9 AM EST, (701)-801-1211, pin: 674-347-093#. I began to listen to the calls every day, and day by day I would come out of that dark place. Two years later with having great success in business, I decided to take my recent notes and write a book to inspire the world that if you would just make a decision, you can win also.

 "Nothing is impossible if you believe."-Tammy Price

ACKNOWLEDGMENTS

Coach Stormy Wellington and the entire Wake Up & Win Team thank you for all of your pouring, giving, and serving, it will not return to us void. This book is a direct reflection of all that you do for us on a daily basis.

W. U. A. W

Chanita Foster- "Girl I'm not tripping, I'm depressed."
Pam McCray- "You are created for greatness."
Larissa Barclay- "Find your lane, stay in your lane, and burn rubber."
Tanya Roquemore- "God's got your back."
Stormy Wellington- "We F.I.G.H.T"

Thank you to Andrea Bracey, CEO of The Educator's Call, LLC for assisting with vision consulting and editing services.

"God Bless!"- Tammy Price

TWTT Enterprises

INTRODUCTION

Have you ever been in a place of depression, hurt, lack, and brokenness, and did not know how you would come out? What if I told you that there was a woman by the name of Stormy Wellington, who was once where you are? She was able to speak and affirm her way out of her circumstances, simply because one day she decided that she no longer wanted to feel those feelings anymore. She understood that it was time for her to WAKE UP & WIN. Well, ladies and gentlemen that woman is now a Visionary and a Multi-Millionaire who inspires thousands of men and women all around the world. I am one of those thousands that she has inspired, and it all started with a daily phone call and a decision that I would no longer settle. There is power in a made-up mind! There is power in your thoughts! There is power in your purpose and in your pain! There is power in the way you affirm things over your life. This book, in conjunction with the Wake Up & Win call will truly help you to win. Get excited because you are now going on a 30-Day journey to Wake Up & Win.

CHAPTER ONE

Change your Conversation

Day 1

Affirmation: "I will hear the voice of the Holy Spirit within."

The best conversation you will ever have is with yourself. Believe it or not, "self-talk" is real. Self-talk is how you got where you are up until this point. My friend you must understand that life and death lies in the power of the tongue, Proverbs 18:21.

You are one conversation away from a complete shift in your life. When you make a decision to wake up and win, you must have a conversation with yourself, begin to visualize, imagine, and see yourself where you desire to be. Your thoughts become feelings, then actions, and finally results.

You mean to tell me that I can stand in the mirror and tell myself "I am powerful" and I will be? Yes, that is exactly what I am saying, which leads me to the next day of your winning process.

Day 2

Affirmation: "I will lead and not follow."

The things you speak, you become. In the beginning God said, "Let there be light," and it was, Genesis 1:3. That is just one illustration showing you how powerful your tongue is. It is very imperative that you begin to affirm over yourself and your life every single day.

It is a battle to stay positive at times because life experiences and challenges can be difficult; however, you must challenge yourself to know WHO and WHOSE you are and begin to speak the very thing you desire out of your mouth. This creates frequency and energy, which ultimately produces results.

You are probably saying to yourself, "I know the power of my tongue, but HOW can it produce results??" If you are in a very dark place right now, and you know that things will get better, just not sure when, as you are on your journey of "things getting better', you must begin to SPEAK LIFE. You have already overcome, you just need a little encouragement along the way. And there is nothing more POWERFUL than someone encouraging themselves.

Day 3

Affirmation: "I will create and not destroy."

Wake Up, realize, recognize, and KNOW that today is your day. We truly become the things we think of, so grab a hold to the power within because God has given you total control and power to have a mental shift.

I believe we become the things we think of, so it is critical to have an internal conversation with yourself to change your thoughts, change your mind, change your attitude, and change your outcome by changing your speech. Your thoughts and conversations go hand and hand. When you change your conversation, you change your life.

If you think you are a millionaire, and you begin to speak it every day, the world will begin to open up to you.

Guess what? Before you know it, you will be a millionaire.

Day 4

Affirmation: "I am a force for good!"

Do you honestly think that millionaires sit around and gossip about people? I don't believe that that they do; it depends on the person. Most millionaires are constantly speaking life, affirming, coming up with ideas, planning, growing, focusing, and continuing to develop their craft to maximize every opportunity they have.

Coach Stormy Wellington used the following illustration…. "Imagine sitting in church service and while the preacher/pastor or speaker is teaching, you begin to zone out and begin to think thoughts like: man, I'm hungry, oh I have to wash, man I forgot to take the meat out, shoot I have five minutes, what time are we getting out of here?" Before you know it, your body is in service, but your mind is somewhere else. Tap yourself and get back focused on the preacher.

We know you can relate but the motive behind this illustration is to show you that you had a conversation in your head and if you would take that same energy, put a plan together and tell yourself "I need to start this business; I need to flip this; I need to lose 30 pounds this month; I need to start reading; let me pawn that tv that I don't watch, let me change my circle.

You can begin to apply those thoughts, boss yourself around on every level, and THEN you will begin to see yourself WINNING.

Day 5

Affirmation: "I defy the odds!"

Subconscious vs Conscious.

Subconscious mind always has a conversation. It is very important to protect your ear gates! Your mind is not completely aware, but it influences your actions. Having a conscious mind is being aware of your thoughts, identity, attitude, and belief. Now, go forward and understand that you are truly in control.

Most mornings I listen to my gospel, and I set the tone for my day, then a few hours later I turn on some rap music, which means it's time to get some money. This shows that what you allow in your ears can affect your mood and outcome. Junk in, junk out. Love in, love out. Peace in, peace out. Give in, give out. Happy in, happy out- just like that.

Day 6

1. Who are you talking to? **Take a moment and examine who you hold conversations with and reflect.**

2. **What** are you telling yourself? **Examine whether you have been speaking life or defeat.**

3. What are your dominant thoughts? **Remember thoughts become things.**

Day 7

Affirmation: "I am a leader!"

Does this conversation....

1. Make me money? **Think of ways these conversations you have helped create income for you.**

2. Make me smarter? **Explain how your conversations have provided you wisdom or knowledge around your goals and/or vision.**

3. Draw me closer to God? **Take a moment and think about how each conversation has helped you spiritually.**

CHAPTER TWO

Exposure

Day 8

Affirmation: "I am the head and not the tail."

Reality is you don't know what you don't know, you think you know but you have no clue. So, how do you know what you don't know? You grow! You grow based on your level of exposure. It's imperative to expose yourself to people on another level than you are. To get further in your life and business, you must force yourself to get in good and fertile environments. Here are four ways to expose yourself to greater: good audios, books, events, and affirmations. It helps you to think on a higher level.

Day 9

Affirmation: "I am above and not beneath."

Do you really know who you are? You are amazing. You have gifts, talents, dreams, power, and purpose waiting to be awakened. I believe you have been sleeping on yourself far too long. You are valuable and deserving of everything your desire.

Stop being cheap with yourself. Invest in you, you are all you have. Constantly remind yourself that you can do better and be better. Don't settle another day with anything or anybody that will cause you to belittle yourself or think small.

Day 10

Affirmation: "I am the lender not the borrower."

Have you ever felt the feeling that something is missing? Maybe you told yourself, "I know it's more for me to do." There is a constant tug at you that won't seem to leave you alone. I challenge you to pay attention and allow that feeling to speak to you.

Don't ignore it any longer. That feeling will begin to destroy your comfort zone. Settling in your ways will make you forget how valuable you are. Allow that feeling to make you want to find out what it is that you are needing to do.

At this point, most people will pray on it, even attend church service, maybe reach out to a friend or a close family member. This is great, but you can't just keep limiting yourself to just doing those things. The internet is a whole world within itself that is open to you, so use it. Discover different events in your local area besides just church service. Change the mundane rituals. Pull up different audios on YouTube. Personal development will make a major difference in your thought and winning process.

Day 11

Affirmation: "I am loved by God!"

There's a difference between exposure and experience. Exposure is education, and experience is your resume. Experience is what you have been through to get to this point. Exposure is the opened door for what your future will hold.

Once you've been exposed to something no one can take it back. Go for your exposure, you can't get there just sitting here. You can't get there with the same average people. You need new people; you will either serve your way or pray your way. I believe if you hang around five broke people, you will be the sixth one.

So, why not pay or serve to hang around four rich people? You become who you hang around. It's not by coincidence you are around these people; it's not by coincidence you are at events with powerful people, but whatever you believe is right!

Day 12

Affirmation: "I am chosen by God!"

Study what you believe to be true. Reading is significant; it allows your mind and thinking to be enhanced. Knowledge is power so use it to your benefit. If you haven't read "Think and Grow Rich" and "The Four Agreements", I encourage you to do so.

While exposing yourself, don't be afraid. Yes, it can be very intimidating to start doing things and hanging around new people. Especially, if they are on a higher level than you. But! If you want something that you never had, you must do something that you have never done. This will take you to a place that you have never been.

Day 13

Affirmation: "I am protected by God."

The world will begin to open up to you as you allow yourself to be open to new things. Awareness takes place in not just sight, but in vision. It's important to also ask questions; you have not because you ask not.

For example, if someone is making 20K a month and you desire to experience that type of income, it is up to you to ASK them questions such as: "What books are your reading, what mindset are you in, what business did you start, how disciplined are you?"

When you are in alignment, you begin to have clarity on the very thing that has been tugging at you! Before you know it, that same 20K you were asking about will be YOURS!

Day 14

Affirmation: "No weapon formed against me shall prosper."

1. Who are you connected to? **Remember exposure is key.**

2. Have you prayed about your feelings? **Awareness begins internally.**

3. Has your EGO gotten in the way? **Have you been edging God out?**

Day 15

Affirmation: "Every tongue that rises against me in judgement shall be condemned."

1. What books are you reading? **If you have not been reading any books, what do you plan to read?**

2. What events do you plan to attend? **Go where you see yourself.**

3. What audios have you listened to? **Remember nothing is coincidental.**

CHAPTER THREE

Are you happy?

Day 16

Affirmation: "I am a champion."

To wake up and win, you must choose to be happy. Happiness is an inside job; it is a choice and a decision that must be made every day.

Rule #1-never put your happiness in stuff. Tangible things or stuff can be gone today and/or tomorrow, but your happiness is internal. Material things are an extra blessing that makes you grateful for the low times and broke days. They are just an addition to your happiness, not the reason you are happy. Everyone's happiness is designed by something different.

I encourage you not to be 'fake' happy, be happy in real life. Don't just smile on the outside, while you are crying on the inside. Repeat after me... "I choose to be happy."

Day 17

Affirmation: "Everything I touch turns to gold."

Our greatest challenge will be our greatest reward. The greater the challenge, the greater the victory. Life's challenges can be painful. We all have experienced loss, disappointments, lack, issues, temptations, anger, insecurities, and hurt.

Me personally, I lived a young life of pain; however, I have learned that I am in control. I'm not in control of what happens, but I am in control of how I react or respond to it.

Begin to speak this, "I refuse to allow this situation or circumstance to kill me!" You must learn to not focus on the challenge but focus on the victory. You deserve happiness and once you grab a hold to your happiness a shift will come.

Choose to turn it around; I know it hurts but make a decision to look at it differently.

Day 18

Affirmation: "It's my season!"

Let nothing and no one stress you out! Choose to stress less. I know you do everything for everybody else, but it is time for you to make sure that you are good. Do not make any excuses for stress… Larissa Barclay said, "You can't take the bills with you." So live while you are living, rise early, decrease anxiety, take a deep breath, and don't worry about anything.

Matthew 6:34 says "therefore do not worry about tomorrow, for tomorrow will worry about itself; each day has enough trouble of its own."

Repeat after me… "I choose me!" The man that angers you controls you, so replace all negative energy and thoughts with happiness…count it all joy and know that it's all working together for your good. Romans 8:28

Day 19

Affirmation: "It's my turn!"

You can have joy, and you can be happy. The best thing to do is come from a level of appreciation vs expectations. Be grateful for everything. No one owes you anything, so do not expect anything. Your expectation should only be in God. Psalm 42:5.

Wake up and be thankful for the simple things in life like air, water, pillows, sight, food, health, and strength. Having gratitude helps place things in perspective.

Asking permission to eat is not fun at all, but whatever state that you are in, be thankful because there's always someone else that is worse off than you.

Day 20

Affirmation: "I am humble."

Operate in your gifts and remember to smile. There's power in your smile. It shifts your feelings. Next time life throws a curve ball, just start smiling and watch how that burden will go from heavy to light.

Not only should you smile, but you should laugh as well. Remember, laughter is good for the soul. Confuse the enemy and change the rhythm. How?...

When you experience a disappointment, just laugh, no more arguing. Do not fuss back and forth, just relax, smile, and laugh. Another thing, I promise you this, if you give, you will receive. Give a smile and you will receive one.

Learn to live life in the moment to embrace happiness. Pay attention to the moment and just BE. The 'moment' matters, can you handle it?

Day 21

Affirmation: "I AM HAPPY!"

Philippians 4:8 "Whatever is true, whatever is honorable and worthy of respect, whatever is right and confirmed by God's word, whatever is pure and wholesome, whatever is lovely and brings peace, whatever is admirable and of good repute; if there is any excellence, if there is anything worthy of praise, think on these things."

Keep your thoughts pure, feel good about yourself, and set goals. Learn to live and love. Most of all, a major key to happiness, is self-love. To be happy, you must take care of yourself. Give yourself good food, water, lotion, a haircut, a new wig, pedicure and manicure, exercise, and take great nutritional supplements.

Accept all your flaws and value your health. "Self-love is the best love." When you understand that the person in the mirror matters most, then you will be happy. No one can make you happy like you. Not a man, a woman, a preacher, or a teacher, but YOU!

If you're happy and you know it, clap your hands!!

Day 22

Affirmation: "I am wealthy."

1. What makes you happy?

2. Are you happy?

3. List three things that you are grateful for?

Day 23

Affirmation: "I am strong."

1. What challenges caused you to alter your happiness? **There is purpose in your pain.**

2. Do you really love yourself? **This question is between you and yourself, be transparent, do not just put yes or no, really look within.**

3. What brings you joy? **Think on those things that truly make your heart smile and bring you peace.**

CHAPTER FOUR

Next

Day 24

Affirmation: "I will never be broke another day in my life."

Repeat after me... "I got next."
Repeat after me... "I AM next."
Repeat after me... "My best is my next!"

The definition of next is coming immediately after "the time or season." In order to wake up and win my people, you must refuse to remain the same and in the same place. It's time to grow and go. Move from ordinary to extraordinary. Go from the familiar to unfamiliar. Familiar is average and ordinary; it will hold you back, it's what you are used to, it's what you can see, it's a comfort zone. It is relaxed, easy, comfortable, and it is the opposite of faith.

Unfamiliar is not known or recognized. It's strange, foreign, new, and it is different. Unfamiliar stretches you, preparing you for purpose.

Day 25

Affirmation: "My dreams and goals are coming into reality, how they will get done is not my business, it's God's business."

Pam McCray says God didn't create no mess. I don't care what it looks like, there IS a next for you, so believe yet for an appointed time. Get in position to activate that thing to be your best and let nothing take you off your game. To be prepared for your next, you will have to let some things and people go.

Against all odds, you must position yourself, set some expectations, keep it 100% real with yourself, and just close your eyes so that you see and visualize where you're going from a spiritual eye, knowing that what's coming is better than what's been.

Day 26

Affirmation: "I am created for GREATNESS!"

When you realize it's time for your next, you could possibly experience fear or become afraid because it's unfamiliar, but Tanya Roquemore uses a powerful illustration, and I challenge you to do this also. Follow me.... She looked at a childhood picture, while staring at her four-year-old self, she asked the child are you okay with your next? She wanted to know if that child was okay with her today in the present moment. The child's eyes were bright, full of expectations for tomorrow, full of life; she had dreams and goals.

So, as you look at your childhood picture, what does he or she think of your right now? The child wasn't afraid of her next, matter of fact she created her next. Yes, she made mistakes along the way, but the child kept going. It isn't over, go talk to yourself, live with it, and do something about it.

Day 27

Affirmation: "Nothing is impossible, if I believe."

My mom died when I was nine years old. I never knew my dad or saw his face. I desired to meet him and my unknown family all my life. So, I looked for him. Trusting that one day, I would see his face. The problem was that I didn't know who I was; I was trying to continue to identify with myself. I believed that I shall have what I said, so I spoke every day, "Lord let me see him." I knew in my heart there was a 'NEXT' for me. I knew that it was more for me to do. I knew that I was born to win even while feeling like a loser.

I persevered through my discouragement and voids. I begin to look more and more, I found him in 2014. God brought him to me; I experienced my NEXT.

The very thing that I desired my whole life happened; I received love like no other and closure of scars I thought would never heal. One year later, in 2015, he died; the last thing my mom told me before she died was, "I will always be with you." The last words my dad spoke to me was, "Tammy, 'Move Forward'", NEXT!

Day 28

Affirmation: "I will live the fullness of life and all God has for me."

From the words of Coach Stormy Wellington, repeat after me... "somethings in my life are about to change." Every single time you are elevated, you were probably hurt first. Its apart of the process. New beginnings are here, and TODAY is YOUR DAY.

It's more than enough money out here, it's more than enough love out here. It's more than enough energy and vibrations, it's more than enough people for all of us.

To thy own self be true, no validation is necessary in your next. Begin to grow through things and realize you deserve the very best. So, tell your circumstance, Next; low income, Next; broken-heart, Next; anger, Next; overweight, Next; unforgiveness, Next.

You can't worry about it; command your day and speak life every single day. It's up to you to Wake Up and Win. -TWTT

Day 29

1. What is your next?

2. Are you preparing for your next?

3. What is the single most important thing that you must accomplish in your life?

Day 30

Affirmation: "I am in a constant state of attracting all the good that I deserve and desire."

List 10 things that you do daily to wake up and win.

1.

2.

3.

4.

5.

6.

7.

8.

9.

10.

Made in the USA
Lexington, KY
04 December 2019